Deeply meaningful poetry for very Serious People

Deeply Meaningful
Poetry
For Very Serious People

Words by Dulsi Ada Corum
Lettering and Images by Gwyneth Hibbett

WATLEDGE BOOKS

First published in Great Britain by
Watledge Books
Copyright © 2019 Dawn Abigail & Gwyneth Hibbett
All rights reserved

ISBN: 978-1-78996-015-0

Contents

This book is dedicated to steampunk and SF author, David Wake.

Mainly because he hates poetry...

My underwear's quite funky too

Stripy Socks

The meetings called
The delegates bustle
Coffee's drunk, amidst the hustle
We sit to talk
They make their stand
To seek approval for their grand plan
And I am wearing
stripy socks

My suit is on, I'm looking smart
The Chairman calls
For our minds, our hearts
Our brains are stormed
Plans are made
I even think I might get paid
But I am wearing
stripy socks

Truth told I am a colourful soul
But to earn my pay
I keep decorum
Wear sombre grey
To appease the forum
Put my costume on to start the play
My suit is dull, but my ankles rock
For I am wearing stripy socks

You try finding a rhyme for
"etheric beam locators"

SYMPATHY FOR THE DALEK

THE ENEMY WE LOVE TO HATE
DOWN CORRIDORS THEY LIE IN WAIT
THEIR HEAD RESEMBLES A BALD PATE
ON WHICH THEIR IDEAS ILLUMINATE
WITH THEIR BUMPS THEY ETHERIC BEAMS LOCATE
THEIR DEADLY RAY GUNS FIRE STRAIGHT
AS THEIR EVIL ACTIONS THEY NARRATE:
"SEEK - LOCATE - ANNIHILATE!"
PUNY HUMANS THEY BERATE
BEFORE THEIR CITIES THEY OBLITERATE
(ARE THEY DRIVEN BY HAND ENVY?)
THEY GLIDE ABOUT, AS IF ON SKATES
AND WE ALL KNOW HOW THEIR VOICES GRATE:
EXTERMINATE! EXTERMINATE!

PITY ABOUT THE SINK PLUNGER

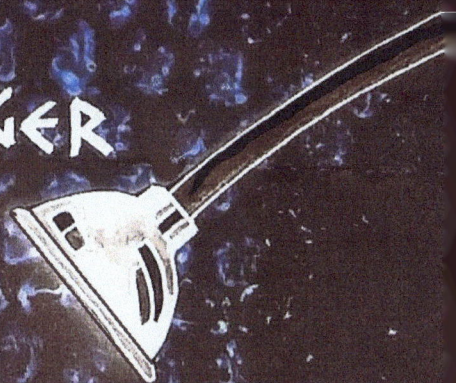

Did you think it was full of beer?

Ode to a Dead Slug I Found Drowned
in a Bucket of Water One Morning

Oh Dead Slug!
You were found
Drowned
In a Bucket of Water
Which means you shouldn't oughta
Climb into fluid bearing containers if you are not entirely sure of their contents.

I'm all for rational dress, myself

YOUR BUSTLE IS LIKE A BUTTRESS

YOUR TEENY HAT INSPIRES ME

Your Corset Doth Inflame

BUT YOUR BUSTLE IS LIKE A BUTTRESS

Defending against my claim

Oft we have conversed

YOUR HAND I'VE HELD IN MY SWAY

But your buttress of a bustle

FRANKLY, GETS IN THE WAY

If I am to win your heart

YOUR MASONRY I MUST DEFEAT

So I'll batter all your buttresses

Until you fall at my feet

Spooky Blokey

My boyfriend is a vampire
That may sound strange to you
But when he shrivels up in sunlight
I know it must be true

My boyfriend's skin is very white
He's long and pale and thin
He has a glass beside his bed
To keep his long fangs in

My boyfriend doesn't drink people's blood
He drinks Guinness instead
He says he needs the iron in it
Because he's really dead

My boyfriend has a pet bat
It's name is "Auntie Lil"
And when boyfriend goes out to play
Bat will go as well

My boyfriend is not really wierd
He's just got a strange idea of style
And he only bites people's throats out
Every once in a while

atishoo!

Ode to Dust

Dust, I hate you
You get up my nose
If only you knew,
How much you, I loathe.
You make my eyes water
And dirty my toes.
You itch my nose
Till nothing grows
in my brain, dust.
If I could trust you to
be good
I would
But I can't

But not the Albion

Angels over Aston Villa

Not a clear blue sky but clouded grey
The day I saw the Angels over Aston Villa
I wanted to go with them,
 they wanted me to stay
"Your time is not yet done" they said
"Now off you go. Away!"
As I sit by the window in the dreary nine to five
Where I sometimes have to kick myself
 to check I'm still alive
I often ponder on the mystery
 but still I don't know why
There were Angels over Aston Villa

What were we thinking?

D·I·Why?

My plaster has gone lumpy
It's cracked upon the wall
There's grit all up the stairs
And dust throughout the hall
That's right – it's D·I·Y

The kitchen diner's getting
A multi-speckled floor
But that's just where we've spilled
Paint destined for the door
That's right – it's D·I·Y

We've papered the lounge carpet
With a maché of scraps
Lining that's eluded
Attempts to stick it back
That's right – it's D·I·Y

To the garden we escape
From the chaos inside
Wondering what we've damaged
Apart from our pride
Tea-break done, we face each other
Two mouths, one voice scream "Screw it!"
Next time it's D·I·Y – someone else can do it!

More tea, Professor?

For the LOVE of TEA

Oh luscious draught!
Oh milky brew!
To drown in an Ocean of your Brownian motion
is all I want to do

But tragic case — your joys I must shun.
Not for me the dried pearls of Assam.
For myself a fragile flower I be
My stomach, alas, too delicate for tea.
Your caffiene would thrill me, your tannin revive
But I must eschew you if I am to survive —
So let me away to a secluded bower
Where I'll sip at a redbush and silently cower.
Shunned by my clan, no duelling for me
As I sadly decline a nice cup of Tea

And that's good enough

Simply Be

What do I want to be?

AN ACTOR? Not that needy

An academic? Not that nerdy

An Acrobat? Not that bendy

AGENT – PROVOCATEUR? Not that trendy

Asymmetric? Not that geometric

So what do I want to be?

Me

To say nothing of the pixies

Something was wrong
It was just the way the Speedwell Road
got shorter every time I walked down it
It got so bad it started to contract under my feet
And the concrete crept insidiously over the grass
Lawns laid heaped up over the pavement
Refugees forced out by the concrete
Moseley crept up to Balsall Heath
and ate it in an off-guard moment
And the only escapees were the unicorns
from Calthorpe Park

ZZZZZZZZZZZZZZ

I LOVE BED

Bed is warm
bed is fun
Bed is for everyone

Bed is soft
bed is white
Bed is with you through the night

Bed is lovely
I love bed
Unless, of course, there's a sofa instead

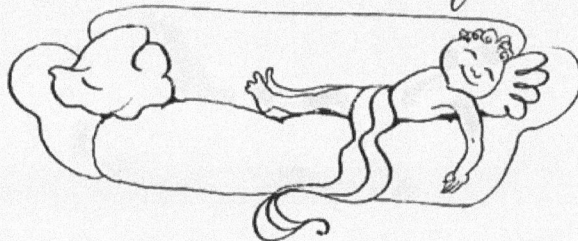

Just so long as he
can take the tops off jars

WIMPS

I think wimps are rather nice
Their legs are long
Their muscles small
They haven't any guts at all
Their shoulders sag
With rounded backs
Their ribs stick out
Just like toast racks
Their smile is mild
They can't be called butch
And most girls don't seem to like them much
But I think wimps are nice

When teaching toast to fly,
why does it always want
to butter the carpet?

ODE to MR TONG

Some days you just lose.

Out of bed, but the side's all wrong
it's the way, isn't it? All along.

YOUR HAIR'S A MESS, YOU WONDER WHY

Your bra is reaching for the sky

Of "those days", you know it's one

Tell Pete it's all gone....
up the inlet, but where's
the paddle?

AND NO RESEMBLANCE
TO THE SHAPE OF AN apple

Some days you just lose.

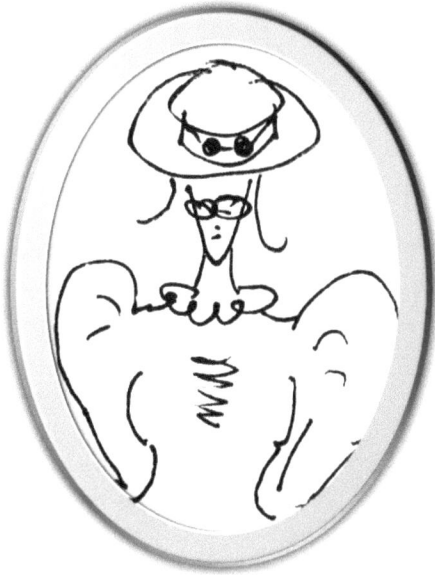

Dulsi Ada Corum has been channelling the eternal spirit of the human condition into humble words since the Dawn of Time. Poetess, Visionary and Fashion Icon, she is also entirely imaginary.

www.dawnabigail.co.uk

@Dawnthepoet

Gwyneth Hibbett is a calligrapher and illustrator with a provisional poetic licence.

www.pen–gwyn.com

Children's Books by Gwyneth Hibbett

Whiskery Tim and the Worry Balloons

The Eagle Eye Detective Agency Series

The Illuminated Oracle
The Mystery of the Disappearing Uncle
The Antiquarian's Problem
The Case of the Missing Agent
Doctor McArdles' Diary